UNQUIET THINGS

Goat Island Poets
Claudia Emerson, Series Editor

UNQUIET THINGS

poems

James Davis May

LOUISIANA STATE UNIVERSITY PRESS
BATON ROUGE

Published by Louisiana State University Press
Copyright © 2016 by James Davis May
All rights reserved
Manufactured in the United States of America
LSU Press Paperback Original
First printing

Designer: Michelle A. Neustrom
Typefaces: Whitman, text; Cinta, display
Printer and binder: LSI

Library of Congress Cataloging-in-Publication Data
are available at the Library of Congress.

ISBN 978-0-8071-6261-3 (pbk.: alk. paper) — ISBN 978-0-8071-6263-7 (pdf) —
ISBN 978-0-8071-6262-0 (epub) — ISBN 978-0-8071-6264-4 (mobi)

The paper in this book meets the guidelines for permanence and durability of the Committee on Production Guidelines for Book Longevity of the Council on Library Resources. ∞

For Chelsea

CONTENTS

The Reddened Flower, the Erotic Bird 1

I Fringe Tree 5
   Portrait of the Self as Skunk Cabbage 6
   Dispute 8
   Lessons 9
   Time for Such a Word 10
   The Reality Auction 11
   Displacement 13
   Protestant Elegy 14
   If You Want the Truth 16
   Sharpened Skates 17
   The Problem with Poems That
      Describe Love 19

II It Only Brings Me Sorrow 23
   To My Lover's Ex-Husband 25
   Fields and Ledges 26
   Basil 28
   Nostos 29
   Reciprocal 31
   It Must Have Been the Mussels 34
   An Explanation of Romanticism 35
   My Keats Year 37
   Late Coleridge 38
   Unquiet Things 39
   One Pearl 41
   Esteesee 44
   Reflections on Having Left a Place
      of Employment 46

III Two Angels 51
    The Crypt on the Rock 53
    Birkenau 54

       Gratis 55
       American Irony 56
       Saint Lucia 57
       Domesticity 59
       Oysters 60
       "A Culture" 61
       L'Origine du Monde 63
       At the Artists' Colony 64
       Natural Grief 66
       The Sap Gone Out 67
       Butterfly Soup 68

IV After Bashō 71
       The Causes of Saints 74
       An Existential Bear 76
       Smerdyakov with a Guitar 77
       Duel 79
       A Variation on the Same 81
       Reverberations 83
       Someone Takes a Pine Tree Apart 84
       Critique and Rebuttal 85

CODA A Lasting Sickness 89

ACKNOWLEDGMENTS 91

UNQUIET THINGS

The Reddened Flower, the Erotic Bird

Out running one morning in early October, at the top of a hill,
I found myself ten feet from an owl perched on a fencepost.

In its beak, a thick cord of taut tissue still attached to the squirrel,
which twitched beneath the talons until the owl, seeing me, dropped it—

and we stood, staring at each other through the cold, barely lit air.
I have told this so many times, but no one, I understand, will understand

the original rapture (yes, I'll use that word) of that moment.
Do we report stories like these—my mother calling me

to say she and my father saw a white ("Not an albino!
It had brown eyes") deer in their yard; or Chelsea, almost breathless,

keys still in her hand, describing the sprinting shadow of the coyote
she may or may not have seen but is pretty sure she had

near the train tracks less than a mile from our house—
do we report them because they are stand-ins, almost,

for grace? And what cynicism keeps me from saying
that we do so because we love, and are surprised by, the world?

Fringe Tree

       —Or *Old Man's Beard*.
That the names we give recall the thing
is what we want. And yet, both names are boring
when compared to the way it shimmers there
like a firework that somehow doesn't fall,
or the way it will fall eventually
from itself, swirling its gauzy pollen
in the wind above the lawn
where the children next door run outside in late April,
swearing to their mother that it's snowing.
And even after they know they're wrong,
they squeal, insisting their mistake
is something to dance through, something
to repeat and repeat again—not hoping
to make it right, just enjoying what it is
and what it looks like the more they say so.

Portrait of the Self as Skunk Cabbage

Maybe it's like those hard
red rubbery spathes
that in early spring—
make that late winter—
create their own heat
and halo themselves
with soil wet
from the snow they melt,
a few degrees of advantage
the plant makes for itself,
like its putrid odor: something
that almost survived the winter
but didn't, convincing
enough to court the thawed-
out insects, those first
mindless urges of life.
Dumb from winter's boredom,
my brother and I
trudged the frost-crusted creek mud
in the woods behind our house
to where the stems
unfolded a too-bright green
we hated because it was ugly,
reminded us of nothing
but itself and thus
reminded us of ourselves.
A presence we wanted gone.
So we slashed it down
with hockey sticks—
each gash releasing the oils
that made those rancid leaves

more rancid. Each year,
the same ritual, the same
erasure of something
that we didn't know
we couldn't erase.
The plant, I found out
years later, grows downward:
the roots pull the stem
deeper into the soil, too deep,
a gardener told me,
to kill it even if you wanted to.

Dispute

Just because you say there was a scorpion in the bed
doesn't mean, the hotel manager tells you,
that there was one in the bed. Nor does it mean
you deserve another room. This is an old dispute,
and winning isn't winning since any claim you make
makes another claim that you're a liar. Add detail,
say, a cufflink, or the precise angle the sun hit the other noun,
and you're too earnest, like the child coming up
from the basement to ask his parents
if they've ever noticed how the coffee table is broken;
he leaves, he returns, reports that in trying to fix it
he broke it more. The worry that every telling
is a form of mangling. A morning in June
when your love still sleeps in the house you step outside of
and into the light before the dawn, the light
that wakes the birds you can't see in the Rose of Sharon—
that "that" that you know better than to describe. You swear
the scorpion was there—your clumsy hands (one in a shoe)
smashed then flushed the real thing into a useless,
unidentifiable abstraction. It makes you wonder
what you really want. But then the hotel manager tells you
"The customer is always right," her fingers fashioned
into ironic quotation marks around the foot-long pocket
of empty air in front of her. She sighs. And at last you can move.

Lessons

My mother kept a few pennies in the ashtray,
which she would throw on the car floor
so I'd look for them instead of at the dead deer
we were driving toward. When I rode with him,
my father slowed down and pointed.

Time for Such a Word

Since we can't read the script his plane scrawls—
the contrails winding in on themselves
in thick uncinched knots—his wife
narrates them over the PA,
giving names to the actions:
Chandelle, Split S, Barrel Roll, Snap Roll.
Maneuvers that look like crashes
until the crash begins, which has no violence
in its long straight-line fall, the way some birds,
if we ever saw them die midflight, must seem
to drop into their sudden weight. We don't turn away
from this important failure, nor does she,
saying, *Oh God. Oh God, something's wrong,*
as it splinters into the Ohio.
The numinous last movements still there
like a child's frantic scribbling held up
as we're asked to guess what it is.

The Reality Auction

(From a typo on a sign in Warne, North Carolina)

It was a dour crowd that gathered at the auction house
beside the Community Center,
elderly, for the most part; the auctioneer, meanwhile,
sounded more like a Latin teacher
rehearsing declensions than a derby announcer
as he invited bidding on the first item,
Sparrow Consciousness, which drew only two offers,
though its description promised keen appreciation
for both the lexicon of gravel and the flavor
of windfall seeds on cold February mornings.

A couple—she wore flowers in her hair,
and a threadbare sundress; he, a greasy ponytail,
jeans, and a stain-spackled t-shirt—bid aggressively
on the blue pills of Altered States and went unchallenged.
The afternoon went on. Objective Reality
went for its asking price, not a penny more.
And when it came time to bid on the Ideal,
a burly man hauled in a miniature oak cask,
the contents of which, the auctioneer said,
should be self-evident, so it remained sealed.

The oldest couple there opened the bidding,
remembering their trip to San Francisco in 1948,
the loaf of sourdough they ate one night instead of dinner
(they could afford the travel but not their meals,
so they ate the bread slowly, tearing off pieces
which they fed to each other, leaning on the bakery's wall
before returning to their motel and making love
as cold air scudded in from the bay and surrounded their bed).

They were outbid, though, by a farmer's widow,
and she, in turn, was overcome by a mustachioed man

in a brown suit who appeared to have won
when the auctioneer, his voice excited by then
but quickening to a stop, opened a manila envelope
and, frowning, announced that the minimum bid
had not been reached, that they had to keep going
or the cask would be returned to the warehouse.
By then, everyone's budget was stretched.
Their sole option was to pool their funds
and share the prize. Fist-thick rolls of twenties,
checks, and jewelry all filled the hat they passed.

When the price was reached and the barrel tapped,
they each tasted their thimble-sized share
of the sunset-red liquor, which was unlike anything
anyone had ever had and thus hard to remember
even seconds after—so they all stayed circling the empty cask,
sniffing their empty glasses, trying to describe what they knew
but couldn't name. A few said it tasted bright, citrusy;
others thought bitter and ashy. "Brisk," one said.
"Well worth it," another added, and the rest stood there
in that sort of silence that sounds like agreement.

Displacement

Lightning where fireworks should be,
quick rain drenching toppled lawn chairs,
plaid blankets, our subjunctive ghosts.
We've traded one benign violence for another,
and it occupies us enough to create wants.
How, for example, to describe rainwater
running down sliding glass doors,
an adjective to address how it's there
and not there, almost a synonym for the word
that should describe the fluid image of a sunlit trout
just out of the shadows and back again.
When my father took me fishing, I'd think
how much the gold, nearly red
bodies submerged in the tea-colored water
looked like functioning but disembodied organs—
living things, but not wholly life. One summer
we watched fireworks from his hospital room.
Not looking at his scar felt like trying
to not look at a woman's cleavage, and I remembered
the nightmare I was about to tell him before he told me
people who tell dreams in conversation are boring.
He was tearing the hook from the fish I held,
its bleeding body stiff as a handshake; the dream
about a voice louder than his yelling at us both.

Protestant Elegy

A Sunday morning in the 1980s,
my brothers and sisters had taken their plates
to the sink, and across the table
my father spread the newspaper,
covering his yellow legal pads and pencils.
The corner of the comics just touched my plate.
I wasn't hungry. I wasn't hungry
because the milk was bad and I knew
I had to drink it. Hard to explain
to a six-year-old why this family of five children—
three from my father's first marriage,
one from my mother's, and then me,
from their marriage to each other—
couldn't waste a thing. I knew only
that I couldn't leave until everything mine was gone.
I thought consuming (though I didn't know that word)
was some sort of demand, an obligation
one had to suffer through to get to enjoyment:
the video game my brothers were playing,
whatever my sisters were laughing at outside.
Saying the milk was bad was useless; we had lied
about almost every meal, said the macaroni
was too yellow, claimed there were veins,
which sometimes there were, in the chalky chicken breasts.
In each sip, a chunk of something, a sourness
that hits me decades later, in July,
when I run past the seafood restaurant's dumpster
or open a months-old Tupperware
full of curry, holding my breath at the sink.
Halfway through the glass, I began to cry.

My father brought it to his nose, sniffed,
poured it down the drain, and came back
with another glass, from another carton,
for me to finish.

If You Want the Truth

Like one of those tired Greek myths
where the punishment seems worse than the sin,
that green heap of shards I shoveled
never dissolved, just grew by the truckload,
the rancid broken edges catching the sun
as they trickled down the slope.

Which is to say my summer job was awful,
and my sin the shame suburban kids get
when they feel the softness glossing their palms.
I remember the long sleeves of molten glass,
the orange stuff some workers dared
the younger ones to skim their hands through,

how we never did, or how one of us did,
and how when Grant lifted his hand
too slowly, it dripped that terrible color
I'd mistaken for the one beautiful thing
in that place, and how he yelled
but never screamed or cried as those men

gathered around him to do nothing
but watch until someone else took him away.
Maybe I wanted the steel mills that closed
before I was born. Maybe there wasn't a war
for me to join or run away from. I asked
almost everyone there if he'd be all right.

The only one who answered said, *If you want the truth,
kid, I couldn't tell you.*

Sharpened Skates

The thumb over the edge, like the tongue
gliding the front teeth when forming
the or *that* or *this* or *then,* doesn't bleed,
not if the edge is sharpened right like this one.

I go back and forth on the metal
as if trying to remember something,
then tilt it to see the thin rainbow veins
in the milky steel, and am drunk

at work again as Russ Morrison
fits the blade to the wheel. With each pass,
burning files spread as his grief would,
if it were visible, from his mouth.

I don't know yet that awful men can do
beautiful things. And at thirty-five,
living with his mother, violent, and—
worst of all—my boss, Russ is awful.

The craft, though, is grind and repetition,
and it's abstract too: a line to follow, a feel,
even a sound like something flying as close as it can
to something else without crashing,

an ideal that we both agree exists
but can never reproduce. So when we look
at the edge we've made, we say *That's perfect,*
which really means *That's close.*

Russ finishes the last pair of skates
and hands them to a kid who watched intently
as the orange brush of sparks flared
and vanished. I'm almost sober an hour later

when, after locking the doors and leaving
the one light on above the red hull
of the sharpener, Russ and I say goodnight,
and I walk home, and he cracks a Molson

for one of the last drives that won't harm himself
and a few others. The air is cold,
but the snow's almost warm, taking back
the tracks he leaves in front of me.

And the boy is on his skates somewhere,
maybe a rink or one of the makeshift pads
behind the old serrated mining houses
that line Squaw Run and Guyasuta.

Either way, the edges cut the ice.
One foot glides, one pushes; snow crests
over the boots when he stops quicker
and better than he ever has before,

so he praises the job of a man he doesn't know
is hurt. Then wonders how it's all done.
The ice is marked. I feel my own edge tonight,
thinking what the boy must have said: *Perfect*.

The Problem with Poems That Describe Love

A long-planned-for day of no plans. We woke
gradually, warm skin warming the other's,

while last night's rain
continued darkening all the new green
we'd failed to comment on during the week.

And after letting Heika out into the backyard
where she scattered the suddenly

legible rabbits to safer places
in the thickening English ivy below the azaleas,

we went back inside to finish our coffee
and the board game from the night before—

all our words making other words.
The strange way the name for a letter

needs more than itself to spell itself.

II

It Only Brings Me Sorrow

Early March in Atlanta, five of us built a fire in the yard and drank as the unseasonably warm day turned into a seasonable evening.

A lot of mud, the few birds still jays and crows.

But the dogwood had complied with the wrong weather: that morning, when Tina arrived unannounced from Knoxville and collapsed, crying on the couch next to Chelsea, I went to the kitchen to make coffee and noticed pale blossoms outside the window.

In the passenger seat of her Honda (a computer program let her record them), fifty or so printouts documenting her husband's online affair, spread out like the losing hand in a poker game.

Even his deletions were noted, a red line through the middle of the letters.

So that night, while she chain-smoked, we undertook the sacred obligation of inventing distractions that don't distract.

After movies and books, Paul transitioned to music, pronouncing bands who fade out their songs in lieu of writing "proper endings" inferior.

I thought of the kids cutting through our hemlocks an hour earlier, how they yelled goodbye back and forth as they parted, not wanting, I think, to be the first not to yell it back.

Then the fading of the day, the bouncing of a basketball one street over getting quicker and quicker from its own dissolving, like I imagine a heart does. Like my father's heart.

And then this gesture: the pinecone someone tossed in the fire, the delicate arrangement of kernels holding as it went from orange to gray to black.

When did we decide, a woman once asked me, not to be friends?

It was an annoying question, and I replied by saying I hadn't thought about it, but I guess right now.

In one email, Tina found her husband deleted *I love you* and instead wrote *I wish I were there.*

Who listens to music—I wanted to ask but didn't—to hear it end?

It's lazy, Paul said—find a note that works and end on it.

He kept on talking like that.

To My Lover's Ex-Husband

This morning, looking behind the bed in the guestroom
as I prepared it for company (you must have stayed there
in the last few nights of the marriage), I found
your vomit, long since dried, spackled
across the wall and relieved of its scent. Which,
from what I've heard, was probably of bourbon
with accents of barley and hops. And yesterday,
as the cardinals lost the feeders to the jays,
Chelsea and I spent a long time ripping the English ivy from the lawn.
We talked about you. The pain you caused her.
Mostly, though, we cursed you for doing nothing
about the ivy when years ago you told her
you were going to do something about the ivy.
You've become, almost, a god,
some genius loci of neglect, indifference, and mistakes.
Yet I know somewhere someone might be thinking the same about me.
The woman I moved to Houston with, married now
to the second bassoonist in the symphony,
no doubt recites my faults. And he has promised himself, and her,
that he will be better than me. And he is.
They probably even have jokes where my secrets—
once promised as secrets—wait faithfully at the punch line.
Or if they're past that, it's because they bonded over talks
about how I hurt her, talked her into moving to the armpit of Texas
only to leave her three months later.
Which isn't true, exactly. But. I scrub the wall.
The water softens this crust and revives for a moment
your bile, its eye-watering stench.

Fields and Ledges

How sweet the pleasures we can't afford
but still pursue. Now that three of them
are finally divorced, four friends
decide to rent a cabin for the weekend.

The one who's never been married thinks
about how fall in North Georgia is not that different
from fall in Pittsburgh. Apples, the coat
you have to wear but feel comfortable in,

the smell—it's more of a rumor, really—
of burning leaves drifting through the bright day,
the reassurance of knowing that someone
still burns them. The wind that brings the sudden

and not quite harmless tantrum of acorns.
Gathering wood for the night's fire, he thinks of his lover,
how at times like the night before,
collapsed and breathing heavily just after sex,

they enter a space where all their jokes,
irony, and default fights don't exist
and all thoughts fail, silently, the way
the hive's worth of bees had died that afternoon

in the cold field—he felt some hit against him
(they were heavier than he thought, muscular)
and drop as if they had just needed the suggestion
of death. Later that night, the woman

who's not his lover drinks gin with five lime wedges
wrung out into the ice cubes crowded
as the stars above them. Her glass
balances on the ledge of the hot tub

like a lighthouse overlooking a green turbulence;
and the three of them, beautiful, naked, and happy
invite him into the water they all call perfect
though no one can stay in it for very long.

Basil

To get him out of the house so she and her husband
can have a few minutes of real arguing, the woman
sends their child out into the garden at night
to pick basil leaves for the tomato sauce she's making.
The boy forgets his flashlight, but knows enough
not to go back inside, plus the moon is bright and full,
filling up the open sky above the yard, like a face
peering over a cradle. The moon, the smell of basil,
how peaceful the house looks when he isn't in it.

Nostos

We had not quite been arguing
that night—but talking, discussing
how I answer any mood of yours
that falls below cheery contentment
with a litany of solutions,
as if trying to help you find
the right word for a crossword puzzle.
Sometimes the heart wants to be sad
and say so and be heard, you said,
or seemed to be saying,
as we followed our dogs out the door
into the yard, the carport light
startling awake at our presence
and then nodding off again.
You'll remember that it was late,
our neighbors hours into sleep,
so we spoke softly even as we began
to really argue, this time
about who locked the door
on our way out. You'll remember
that we gave up our prosecutions
when we realized one of us
had to hold the brittle ladder
while the other climbed to the window
we thought might be unlocked.
Part cat burglar, part narcissistic voyeur,
I paused after unfolding myself
into the room, observing
what we were when we weren't there.
The television, mid-conversation,
prattling on without us; my beer still cold,

unmoved. You'll remember
how the tails behind you wagged,
how happy we were to have back
what we had. I remember
I felt so heroic giving that to you
by just opening the door, which,
I can tell you now, I'm certain I shut.

Reciprocal

She says, *I think you think too much
when you talk dirty.*
                          They are, in fact,
having sex when she says this—
he's above her and had just kissed
the inside of her ankle, which now rests
on his shoulder. He asks what she means.

*I mean, you're too, I don't know,
exact, like you're trying to not sound stupid
even though that's what you should sound like—
you shouldn't be thinking.*

                          He slows down,
almost stops but doesn't.
It's the sort of comment, he thinks,
that would make a passionate person
stop and leave the room, then the house,
viciously dressing while cursing.
He doesn't want to and isn't even
that hurt, more perplexed, really:
how does one make a conscious effort
to become unconscious?

Then that suspicion again that because
he seems incapable of having them,
then the emotional acts of others—
the exhibitionistic weeping
of the woman in the audience at that morning's talk
on the mortality figures in Darfur
and those sappy Lite FM dedications

(probably made by the same people
who clap at the airport when they see soldiers)—
must be, if not lies, then forms of propaganda
intended to usurp what moral credit they can.

But that he keeps making love seems
only further proof of the chronic hollowness
he has made a life of finding and forgetting,
the tragic version of the rabbit hole
he remembers before mowing the lawn
and steps into anyway.

✦

*Talk to me. Talk to me,
baby. Tell me what you want.*

I want the holiness of morning fog, the shock
of imagining a hawk and then seeing one flash by.

No, tell me what you want—

I want my glance from your face
to the restaurant's mirror to be quick enough
to catch me still looking at you.

*Tell me what you want
to do to me.*

I want to do what you want me to do.

I want you to want to do what I want you to do without you wanting to do it because I want you to.

Well, good then, that's exactly what I want too.

It Must Have Been the Mussels

Prostrate, sweating, cheek against the rug,
she moans and waits for him to finish
vomiting into the toilet so she can do the same
again. Years of working their bodies together,
conspiring to feel the same at the same time,
as if a few seconds of shared pleasure
could rescue them from their separate, private,
droning forms of loneliness. So what to say
about this new intimacy? That it's new.
And terrible. That when they think they're done,
they're not. So much tenderness in his holding
back her hair. And when he shits in front of her
while puking into the garbage can—what
comes next? They lie down together and breathe.

An Explanation of Romanticism

We've just had sex, so I'm quiet
and thinking about something else,
looking out at the eastern hophornbeam's flowers,
drooping catkins that are *preformed*, meaning
they grew in the winter bud, independent
of the steady August light, and yet,
fed by it nevertheless:
the stored energy from those summer mornings
working itself into the thing of right now—
and then she asks
what childhood memories make me feel safe.

What follows is a litany of old terrors:
barking dogs, the rolling toy pony I got one Christmas,
the woods, lightning bugs, all bugs, snakes,
my grandfather's vacant mouth, Santa Claus's lap,
the cork wall in my oldest brother's room
and how it slit my fingers open at least twice.

In one of my first poems, I wrote, "I am terrified / of everything."

She asks again, and this time hoping maybe
for hockey memories, adds the idea
that ability can be a type of safety.

And I think of the first time my parents used that word
ability to describe something I did. A story
about how, though three rooms away, I would wake up
as soon as my father woke to use the bathroom, at which point
I'd leave my own bed to take his place next to my mother.

I was still young when I heard this and liked the way,
when telling it, they laughed. My mother never chuckles;
her laughter is sudden and indomitable,
like the explosion of painful expectation and regret
that comes when a roller coaster crests its first hill.

A few nights later, remembering the memory they remembered,
and to please myself by pleasing them, I went
through the dark to their room. But when I got there,
the door was locked. Speaking through it, my father said
to go away. I knocked again. My mother said
I couldn't come in. Not unless I had an absolute emergency.

My Keats Year

Shouldn't it be I'm disappointed *by* (or *because of*) and not *in* you?

We were watching Steller's jays—I didn't know their names then,
I addressed the first one as "Monsieur Mohawk"—watch us,
or watch our meal rather. I don't know if birds feel disappointment,
but as they flitted around the perimeter of the patio
with an odd combination of aggression and timidity,
their feet on the sun-bleached railing
making sounds like a hand searching a filled drawer
for something that's not in the drawer,
the diminishment of cereal must have been processed
as the bird-equivalent of disappointment.

When I picked up Chelsea's bowl and took it inside to the sink,
I thought of California (it was my first time in the state),
and then of Robinson Jeffers,
and then of the time Jeffers realized
he was older than Keats when Keats died, and then I realized
I was older than Jeffers when he realized this.

He was taking firewood back to his house and had to walk over a very narrow bridge, one that his dog seemed reluctant to cross again. So he left the bundle, carried the dog over, and then went back for the wood when he was hit by his age, and then the "insignificance" of what he had written.

And yet we say, "I'm disappointed with myself,"
which sounds redundant.

The woman eating dinner with us the night before told us there was no age she wanted to go back to. Someone pointed out that she was still young.

Late Coleridge

> In their drawing room, they had at one side a mirror that filled an entire wall. When he rose to leave, Coleridge would inevitably start to walk into the mirror.
> —WALTER JACKSON BATE

If it gets to that point and, leaving,
you walk toward what seems the greatest,

most open space, but find instead yourself,
a jowly mess, pale as the settee

where friends flinch on the margin
(one stands halfway up, out of pity,

not sympathy), admit that this stumble
was no mistake but rather a symptom

of that uncertainty you've felt
unfurling in you like a slow sore throat.

The clock, the brass girandole, the thumb-
width flames drilling through wax, all obscured

because you see too much of what you didn't.
Stand there. Breathe. Watch it all cloud over.

Unquiet Things

Well, more and more, I invent new agitations
to keep the old comforts necessary.
The A/C on low while the fire
and expired Vicodin nurse my hangover.
And you drive north. Huge billboards
caption the time-lapse of seasons.
So many zip codes of orange groves.
Then the latitude where the leaves
almost don't fall and the land starts to rise
like a wedding dress's train.
When you get close to Cumming,
someone told me, think of baseball.
Is the little dog in your lap? Your tea cold yet?
Could talking about poetry while you drive
through those stampedes of anxious semis
be the only way for us to make it dangerous?
No Spy Nozy lurking on the peripheral,
putting his ear up against my window
like anti-Jacobin frost; nothing to risk
but failure in front of, what, a few hundred
at best. A lot of blushing because we've blushed.
And if I were sweet to you right now,
my selfishness and chronic forgetting
might make that kindness matter more.
The cake part of the cake, isn't that
what allows us to swallow the too-sweet icing?
So much of what's pointless is needed:
the things that make the other things important.
Southerners, I've noticed, fail to praise warm days.
But I never believed in varying degrees
of geographical compassion

until I left Pittsburgh and realized
that in no place else do people yield
to the first car turning left at the light.
Even in Pittsburgh, when I see this,
I somehow start missing Pittsburgh, how
there are no infinitives there, since too much—
hills, snow, the Ohio—already stands
between what's needed and desired.
So the car needs washed and I want kissed.

And how quickly our distance diminishes
while we talk. Soon you'll pass the huge peach,
the three-story steel one that fills the sky
like a rogue Impressionist moon. My fire,
a thin blue film fluttering on the grate
with the capriciousness of central air.
Which is to say I miss you more
because you're almost here. Which is what
we really want. To balance on edge
like that time you stood on the too-high diving board
and didn't want to jump but had to and did.
Think of baseball. I mean, help. I mean, I need loved.

One Pearl

John Weir! Remember when you used to call yourself
the sodomite at my window? Houston
was so odd. Every mile the same pattern.
A strip mall with a strip club, a school,
then a mansion next to a tire factory—
all repeating themselves like the background
of some Saturday morning cartoon chase.
Before I left, it seemed I was always searching
for someone else's lost dog, nearly falling
on the sidewalk's confusion of acorns.
And Atlanta? No sodomites like you here.
Today the azaleas' birthday-cake pink
materialized suddenly as cards
shooting out from a magician's palm. Wait.
Is that clear? Just understand they're beautiful,
that I'm tired of clarity, of condescending
marble statues, of being tired of being tired.
Tonight's guest speaker quoted a mime
who reportedly said, "One pearl is better
than a whole necklace of potatoes."
A woman nodded, a man made a sound
that sounded like polite pleasure.
And in the cocktail party that follows
all those pretty words, here I am
on the porch, my left ear faintly lit
and half in New York because I kept dropping
cracker crumbs into my wine
and someone asked me if I was Fiction
or Poetry. I'd ask how you are,
but I know you hate yourself and want to die.
Yes, I have stolen much, and in the great circle
of folding chairs crushing the oriental rug,

I've retold the stories and jokes of others
as if my own, seizing the obligatory laughter.
I don't know how one gets away with beauty
or grace or, I worry, how to admire art
without wanting to have made it myself.

But, then again, I know a building downtown
(or the stunted beginnings of one),
which no one's worked on since a storm
gutted the city six months ago; and so,
the structure—it's only beams, no walls—
is open to the wind that lifts and spins
the newly loose things I cannot see
into a peal, a soft desultory chime
like many singular keys falling at once.
And in Krakow, every hour starts
with a broken progression of notes
because, sounding the alarm centuries ago,
a trumpeter took an arrow through the throat.
When I hear it, I feel sad. Though it's awkward.
Though through the acid wash of a migraine
I walked past a group of German students
chanting "Po-tate-o" until they broke
into guttural laughter below the basilica
from which, sometimes, the trumpeter waves.
Maybe the unfinished, maybe the fractured.
Maybe what the friend of the dead poet,
a poet himself, asked: "to forgive so much
that poor obscure-baffled Thing,—
myself."

But the crowd of blazers
and frizzy hair exits en masse, releasing
a puff of rank praise and nepotism
into the midnight air. So I move
toward the dogwood, the goldenrods, the irises,
that, if I could, I'd describe for you,
my gentle-hearted friend, how they all stay
where they are. No, how they all *seem* content.
No, not even that. I'd describe them all
as if it mattered. As if it didn't not.

Esteesee

I have also mistaken strong desire
for talent, and more than once I've watched
as the moth I was pissing on
began to fly out of the urinal toward my face.
But there have also been small triumphs
in small European towns—
cold beer after an afternoon of sex,
my chair teetering on the cobblestones
like a scale's needle. And occasionally
I've been better than exceptional people
who were not quite or no longer at their best.
These moments, I think, matter as much
as the ones that haunt us: sinuous shadows
unfurling their wings in front of you;
my mother steering the station wagon
at the hornets' nest, knocking it down
so they attacked the glass like typewriter hammers,
all for me to learn, she said,
to never disturb one myself.
                              Remember, if things
get too stinking serious, the philosopher advised
taking a bathos. So when my friend, after much
genuine arguing to improve what he found
to be my suspect character, told me, in all seriousness,
that though I was raised by lawyers,
the world itself was not in fact a courtroom,
I gently proved him wrong. But if I were to call
my witnesses, who would speak on my behalf?
Though we returned the wallet, its thick
rainbow of bills was pretty enough
to make me wish otherwise.

                              And I have doubted
the pains of others—undetected,
I watched and waited for the "nerve-damaged hand"
to open the door, and felt like I won something
when it so adroitly did. But if the pain is faked,
doesn't that imply another kind?
And could one sympathize with a man
who suffers from an acute lack of empathy?
No, I have nothing to complain about;
whom I love loves me, and she has never
made me cry over boiling milk
spilt across my leg. And I have friends
who are not here, which is the only way
I can speak to them, tell them all about
the peculiarities of *this* tulip tree's leaf,
how it looks like an incomplete maple's
and does this and that in the wind.
And my lament? Do I need a lament?
I need a lament. I'm so average, even in my failures,
that for years now the only compliment I get
(if I get one at all) is about how I'm still so young.

Reflections on Having Left a Place of Employment

Looking up at the mountain this morning—
gossamer-thin fog drifting in a wind
whose movement somehow makes the stillness
more still, and bold blue hues at the base,
bold as if colored by a painter,
a bad painter who loves the mountain
without irony or sadness
and wants to say just that—I think of my mother
who at this moment sits in a doctor's office
decorated like a spa, hooked to a machine
she hopes will freeze away what little fat she has.
And later, another doctor in another office
will inject paralyzing toxins
into the muscles of her cheeks and forehead
to prevent frown and smile lines.
The family joke goes that my cesarean birth
was the result of minor complications
from a routine tummy tuck.
                          It occurs to me
that I have come by my aestheticism
honestly, the rightful successor
of a family business, which he loathes
and needs because he knows little else.
So when I praise the mountain, understand
that I praise beauty, not nature.
                          Consider
last week: but for my neurotic dog,
I seemed the only one suspicious
of the pumpkin-orange water
shimmering in the swimming hole.
Before I could wade in, a bee stung my foot
and I felt so grateful for the excuse

that I sat quietly on my blanket all afternoon
while the others swam. *I'd call you cold,*
a friend once told me, *but cold is too Romantic.*
And it's true: I've never wanted to bow,
to offer up, and I've learned everything
I need to know about going barefoot
from the bee. Yet, I have been stricken
by the recurring symptoms
of a sincerely overwhelmed heart
and have come to on the kitchen floor,
surrounded by jovial paramedics
and upset that I upset my favorite glass,
not to mention my wife. The first time
I told her that I loved her, I asked her
not to make a big deal about it,
though for months I had been saving
her voicemails. My genial spirits, meanwhile,
have been known to flail when I see a heron
or a close parking spot.
                          No, don't pity
the ugly man who has been taught to love
only beautiful things. Pity the mountain
whose painter loves what he sees, not what's there.

Two Angels

> You are searching for angels but, alas, not very good at finding them.
> —ADAM ZAGAJEWSKI, IN CONVERSATION

But they found me once, two of them.
Both were impeccably dressed in gray
sharkskin suits. It was late, in my basement.
It is very important, the first one said

(hand on my shoulder, pinching it slightly
the way my brother sometimes does to remind me
of some decades-old ass-kicking),
extremely important that you . . . He

set down his glass, went to the dartboard,
retrieved the darts he'd thrown,
and handed them to me. I was tired,
losing terribly. Important that you—Wait,

the second angel interrupted, ask him
if he's happy. Yes, gentlemen, I am happy,
I blurted out. They looked at each other,
then asked for some proof. Well, I am

in love, I said. But they pointed out
that doesn't cause happiness. Often results
in quite the opposite, the second one said.
I threw a dart. I have two dogs,

I have known few tragedies, encountered
few deaths. Both rolled their eyes,
but I continued. I love music. And October,
its moments of benign forgetting, when sometimes

I walk outside into the evenings to thank
your kind employer. Snickering angels
sound like snickering men. I threw the second dart,
perhaps too hard. And at that, they said

they were not there for my impatience. Both rose,
collected their hats and vanished, leaving me
embarrassed and still holding the last dart,
aiming at something only luck could help me hit.

The Crypt on the Rock

> You swore never to be
> a ritual mourner.
> —CZESLAW MILOSZ

My language and friends are behind me now.
A mile down Grodzka, I bought water and cheap bread.
Then on my way to your church's baroque spires,
I passed the historical marker next to the bakery.
And here, in front of you, these red candles
have melted to rings, a day's worth of flowers
piled up on your granite with five unread notes.
The odd, underwhelming feeling of tombs.
Is it from the disappointment of not knowing
what to do? I wait and leave,
heading back what feels like too soon
into the painful sun where three teenagers
smoke at the ankles of some patinated saint
and a jackhammer pummels the sidewalk
into the wrong scene. The want for something
more than this common ugliness. So I look back,
but feel instead my palms, blasted by the pain
of what almost happened, go flat on the car's hood.
The wheels turn. I'm warned in a language
I don't know to watch where I'm going.

Birkenau

An hour into their tour of the death camp,
they lean in to kiss each other, but pull back,
realizing the disrespectfulness of the act.
They weren't intending a long kiss,
just something simple—you're here,
with me, I love you. Thank God for that.
Then in a sort of embarrassed defense,
they start to notice the minor atrocities
of the living: the teenager wearing a shirt
that reads Pills Kill But Guns Kill Better,
children playing tag on the tracks
leading to the gas chamber's rubble
(their parents smiling, taking pictures)—
and then the beautiful sky in the background
that looks like a beautiful sky in the background.

Gratis

Poets are not often rich, but this one was
since he embraced the state, wrote
doctrinal hymns, odes to celebrate
the dictator's birthday, even the dictator's dog.

So when another poet's daughter
went to see this poet—her father, a member
of the Resistance, had been captured
in the woods and sentenced to death—

she did not expect sympathy. But still,
she told him, you're both poets,
and maybe this is worth something
(I don't know if she used a question mark).

I heard this story in the country where it happened.
I was drinking strong coffee. My friend
sipped white wine. Of course the one poet
used his political pull to save the other;

otherwise his reply to the daughter,
Well, what is poetry for but to save lives
(I don't know if he used a question mark either)
wouldn't have been remembered.

Nor would it have survived for decades
in the conversations of so many others
to reach me, who offered to pick up the check
only when he saw it securely in his friend's hand.

American Irony

Tomas tells us how, in Prague, in '68,
he helped to switch the street signs.
After taking one sign down and replacing it
with a sign from across town, he'd walk a few blocks
then relabel another street. Again and again.
A process which he describes as "not inartistic."

Even confusion, he says, has its rhythms and logic:
the Resistance had to give just enough accuracy
to make the invading army believe the false routes.
And it worked. The tanks spent the day
circling back on themselves like lost ants
on a piece of paper that someone kept turning.

But like the schoolchildren who pretended
they didn't know Russian, this tactic only delayed things.
Eventually the soldiers found the radio station and square.
"The intelligent," he says, "opposed things
until it made sense to stop—but the others . . ."
He gulps his drink as if trying to douse the sentence.

And I remember my friends in high school,
how, as a joke one night, we stole three or four
of our own neighborhood's road signs, then panicked
that our parents would find them. Our solution
was to throw them into the creek, like we did our beer cans.
Nothing happened, of course.

Saint Lucia

My beautiful mother
  was ugly, or told as much,
    until she was twelve.

So I inherited a materialism
  that borders on religion:
    The one that costs more

is the better one. Now,
  this summer, we have
    two absurd mountains,

and between them a beach
  with white sand
    imported from Africa.

This isn't some progressive vacation,
  I told you. Sure, there's poverty—
    (I was thinking of what we saw

on the shuttle ride in:
  bony horses, half-abandoned cows
    on short leashes,

people not faring much better)
  but we don't want to see that.
    Not this week. That was at breakfast,

where the stray cats waited
  for the scraps we never gave them.
    You told me you'd never seen a cat

with balls before, and then pointed,
and they were big.

Domesticity

They came back from their honeymoon
and were excited to see that in the absence of their dogs
two cats had moved into the backyard.

Two cats and dozens of small, dead animals.

Oysters

When he lost his job, and a woman
they both agreed was cold and shallow
and grossly privileged, though victimized
in her own mind, got a very, very
good job, and—in the same week—
their close friend's newborn
was diagnosed with a condition
that causes tumors of the eye,
which may or may not blind the child for life,
they went out for oysters and martinis
they couldn't afford and parsed
the indiscriminate distribution
of . . . they couldn't name what it was
they were naming. *Happiness?* No,
they knew the woman with the job
wasn't happy, would never be, but lacked
the inner resources to realize this was so.
Fortune, the wrong word, too, something
from a centuries-old novel
where character names correspond to, well,
character: *Mr. Snide plotted; Mrs. Fairweather
tucked the children in at night.* He suggested
fate or *destiny* but both seemed too mythical.
By then they were on their second dozen;
the blind, shapeless animals lay exposed
on their communal deathbed of ice,
not suffering, the man and woman thought
together but separately, because
the species didn't have the instruments to understand
they were suffering. The drinks were strong,
the world stubborn but scrutable—
all night they searched for a word, as if it would help.

"A Culture"

That's what the voiceover calls the family of orcas,
   because over generations, through language and imitation,
     they have preserved their methods for hunting stingrays.

Approaching its prey, the orca will turn upside down,
   clasp the ray in its teeth and then right itself so the
     ray is upside down, which triggers some evolutionary typo

that floods the ray's brain with serotonin, rendering it
   completely calm before the orca leisurely halves the body.
     It was the sort of image any book would lose to,

no less the sentence I was reading that declaimed *art*
   must be useful. After commercials, another clip, this one
     of a mother protecting her pup by using the same technique

on a great white. Murky shadows in frothing water,
   noises from circling birds and bewildered tourists on boats.
     For fifteen minutes she held the shark belly-up

to the surface so water no longer rushed across the gills.
   A slow suffocation, then flakes of masticated tissue,
     the nutrient-rich liver consumed, and the body left for the gulls.

The book on the table for the night, Chelsea and I
   went to dinner where I failed to make interesting or plausible
     my idea about the orcas—how their language works

like those ancient and useful mnemonic poems about farming
   and laws. *The end of writing,* Johnson said, *is to instruct;*
     the end of poetry is to instruct by pleasing.

We had no idea what to order. Then our French waiter repeated Chelsea's question: "What is the duck stuffed with? Madame, the duck is stuffed with more duck."

L'Origine du Monde

We saw so many people
ignoring the painting—
or rather, we saw so many people
ignoring the painting
because of the labia
featured in the painting.

Realism, Courbet argued,
is not the straightness of lines
nor strictness toward forms
but perception
suddenly composed.

Yet it's hard to describe
pubic hair—chimney clouds rising,
crosshatched shadows?—
and not sound absurd.

Finally, a man walked over to the painting
and put his finger to his chin
before taking a picture. Then
a teenager turned around and smirked
before taking a picture.

At the Artists' Colony

Look at yourself, Mr. Hands-in-Pockets,
married, early thirties, mildly educated,
wearing the evening's sole blue blazer,
watching the nude's shadow pirouette
along the custard-colored curtain
and circle that other shadow,
a male's, who strokes between his legs
the shaft of an exaggerated candle,
making the flame shiver on the wick.
You're upset because you don't get it.
Upset because it makes you uncomfortable
to not get it. Maybe that's the point:
to feel uncomfortable, to feel
as though your little ordered world
is being laughed at. Derided. Or do you still think
that art is insight? That would explain
your version of humility: dispraise yourself
before anyone else can, the dinner host
who bemoans each delicious course
because it doesn't taste as good
as he imagined. Ideals should be yearned for,
not reached. Isn't that sports rhetoric,
that it counts to try and fail? Go Truth!
Clearly, the doormen at the last installment,
clad in all-black nylon body suits
and minotaur masks, were laughing
when they ushered you into the mini-discotheque,
where under the epileptic light
they tried to dance with you
and, when you refused, your wife.
A small audience in the next room,
also laughing, watched through a webcam.

Derided, from the Middle French *derider,*
to ridicule, to laugh at unkindly. Your little world.
Don't you like anything, your wife asks
outside in the courtyard. And you show her
the varnished antique bathtub
packed with soil and verdant with mint
and rosemary. She doesn't say anything,
but that's just the gallery's herb garden.
People, believe it or not, actually live here.

Natural Grief

To see the four crows surrounding the fifth,
the sick one, this morning and all afternoon
as it died on our driveway, leaving its carcass
and a smattering of sun-dried droppings—to see them stay
until one nudged the dead with its beak
and, receiving no response, paused for a moment,
a long moment, before taking a full and what looked like
exaggerated stroke of its wingspan that lifted it away,
an action the others followed. To see
that long vigil through casual and then more frequent returns
to the kitchen window and not think the birds
feel something comparable to our sorrow
would be, I think, a dismissive mistake. Like the phrase
bearable tragedy. Or the condolence *Well, he lived
a long life* . . . I kept hearing at my grandfather's wake,
in the same tone you'd use to justify a bad
but free meal. Three days ago, our neighbor, Jane,
an eight-year-old adopted as an infant from China,
told us she was getting a baby sister, and yesterday,
her arms around our dog, she told my wife
that she and her parents weren't going to China again,
that something went wrong, that her sister's blood test
wasn't right, something she didn't understand.
It's weird, she said, *to be sad about someone you haven't met*.
Jane was left outside a hospital on a snowy night
in December, wrapped in blankets. Her birth parents
cared enough to make sure she'd be found.
The crow seemed to weigh less than the bag
I shoveled it into. When she saw me
place it all in the garbage can on the curb, Jane asked
what it was, and I lied. And then told her the truth.

The Sap Gone Out

We found the newborn possum still wet with afterbirth at the foot of the pines.

Five slick wasps moiling over it, slowly rolling back the tear at its shoulder to get to the leaky purple muscle.

We thought of sickness. We thought of it falling from the upper branches.

Our dog went closer than we did, but not much closer.

By lunchtime, I'd given up trying to build some moral out of it returning to the earth, life feeding death, death feeding life, etc.

The soft meat goes first. No, the salty gel of the never-opened eyes goes first, sipped up like syrup.

And the wasps will die soon too.

That they're eating meat now, as they do in autumn, means that their larvae have grown and no longer defecate the rich paste the adults consume throughout the summer.

Think about it: the adults bring the sugars—saps, nectars, pollens—to their young, regurgitate into their mouths, and then the young, in turn, produce a substance the adults suck out of the larvae.

At some point, we get tired of cycles. All this rebirth.

I wanted to say we yearn for things to simply end when we end. The way my niece thinks she's invisible when she closes her eyes.

But mostly I wanted to describe the possum to you one more time.

So I went outside, only to find something had taken it already, taken it whole.

Butterfly Soup

There's really no grace to their names: Red Peacock,
Green Triangle Kite, Blue and Brown Clipper.
A nomenclature of awkward plainness,
because trying to describe the metallic,
nearly turquoise wings of the Blue Morpho
in two to three words could only end in failure.
Our guide points to one, says it isn't actually blue,
but that tiny scales on its wings scatter the light,
similar to the way dust molecules refract the sun's rays.
When he finishes speaking, the boys in our group
give chase to whatever flutters by them,
while Jane, the only girl, keeps to the trail
that leads down to where the artificial stream
turns to go back through the filter
and we find the shredded fragments of so many wings
like confetti simmering in puddles after a parade.
Or are they more like the fronds and stems of the fruit
Chelsea was cutting for the salad last night?
Her knife slid through the strawberries.
The tiny green leaves, much lighter
than the small amounts of red flesh they clung to,
bobbed in the sink above the apple peels,
melon and orange rinds. I kissed her neck,
said I was sorry for something—it hardly matters what—
and without looking she put a strawberry in my mouth.
We dip our hands in the stream. Jane tells me
butterfly soup probably wouldn't taste very good.
To keep us from eating them, she says, the bright,
beautiful things always have a bitter taste.

IV

After Bashō

Because pointing at the frog
  is enough motion
    to scare the frog away,

a man and a woman
  place a pair of weather-beaten chairs
    by the little stone pond

in the driveway of their rented cabin—
  they are on vacation,
    trying to get pregnant—

and wait, "like Buddhist monks,"
  she says, for the frog
    to reemerge from the pixelated water.

The man has yet to imagine
  his child's face. He's not even sure
    whether he'd prefer a boy

or a girl, and with a feigned
  but private detachment,
    tells himself that any wants

during the process (they may not
  conceive, after all)
    will lead to regret, and since

he can't control things he won't
  worry about them. But
    something about that feels like trying

to will a telephone to ring
    by not thinking about it—
        he used to do that in high school

while waiting for a girl to call,
    and again and again he'd catch himself
        glancing at the phone, or, more often,

he'd wish he were by the phone
    instead of with his parents,
        as on the Saturday night

in late August when his father
    pulled into a field under a clear sky,
        got out of the car, and walked

fifty yards into the waist-high wheat
    to gaze up at the comet
        he'd waited all summer to see.

The man remembers telling his father
    that the purple cloud of light
        looked like a big, beautiful

fingerprint smudge and then asked
    if they could go home.
        Irony, he thinks, was the only way

to hurt his father, and it'll probably be
    the weapon his child will choose
        to hurt him with too—

so he imagines refuting his own child,
   telling him or her that irony
      and sarcasm can't express wonder.

How do you plan to praise? he'll ask.
   And, at what will no doubt
      be rolled eyes or a turned back,

he'll add that there's nothing brave
   in tearing down the world.
      Loving the world, now that's brave.

By now the woman realizes
   her husband doesn't see the frog
      glistening on the rock.

She nudges him, but it's already gone.

The Causes of Saints

When at eighteen weeks
Chelsea went into preterm labor
and to keep our child
had to have her cervix sutured shut,
I sat in a large room
that seemed more hotel lobby
than waiting area—
a two-story atrium window
admitted strong sunlight,
and the stairway's banister
and the crown molding
were both polished cherry.

Mounted high on the wall,
a screen like the arrivals board at the airport
listed each patient's status,
but told me none of the things
I wanted to know.
I still watched with relentless attention.

One summer, my grandmother,
probably to keep me from squirming
under the pews, said
that two weeks before
the church's statue of Jesus on the crucifix had wept.
My job was to watch
and let her know if more tears came.
But for the scarlet,
almost pocket-square red
of the chest wound
and a few brown splotches

that were supposed to be dirt
if they weren't actually dirt,
the plastic skin was completely pale.

I hadn't thought about that
until Chelsea's status changed
from In OR to In Recovery and I saw
her surgeon striding toward me—
the feeling that if I looked away from him,
the miracle that may have happened
wouldn't happen.

An Existential Bear

> Nothing exists until it is observed.
> —JOHN ARCHIBALD WHEELER

The theory is that to perceive something
is to create it, or rather to help to create it.
Until then, those mountains and the trees
drilling through their soil, and the afternoon moon
above them, occur, at best, as probabilities—
that the universe has created beings
to rescue it from that probability into existence.
So by turning to look at it, the old man
on top of another mountain makes Vermont
throw itself together in the July heat
the way individual cartoon bees assemble
into a swarm the moment they realize
the bear has reached into their hive.
The swarm becomes a fist, a pair of scissors,
finally an arrow before the bear concludes
that these are the wrong sort of bees.
Or consider the real bees in the first hours of spring
mobbing the early-blooming plum tree,
the bees my daughter fears, so we tell her
to stand still, *like a statue,* when they approach.
Only two years old, there's not a world
that she can imagine in which she is not seen,
so she flails at each buzz. By evening, though,
we've explained away the fear: she understands
that the bees don't want her, that they want flowers.
"So that they can turn them into honey,"
I tell her. "Yes," she says, "so I can eat it."

Smerdyakov with a Guitar

Tonight I'm thinking
  of my wife's first love
whom I've never met
  and last week was shot
in the head by his coworker
  who shot seven others
and then himself.
  You know the story,
you may even know *this* story.

First week of October,
  a spastic wind outside
shaking moonlight
  off the pampas grass.
The earnest signs
  on telephone poles
warning the neighborhood
  of the coyote pack
that haunts our pines.

I haven't seen one yet,
  but as she inspects the yard,
our dog's hackles spike,
  though she's never seen one either.
And I've never seen
  a man shoot another man,
though I once held a woman
  after she had been shot
through the neck and jaw

and drove back to her apartment
   next to mine. Resilient
is the word the surgeon used
   to describe the brainstem
which controls the heart
   even when everything else
has died. My wife's first lover
   will die tonight. My neighbor
survived, as will the coyotes

who keep to the shadows,
   picking off a cat
or two, toppling trash cans
   to get at the soup bones
sweating through the plastic.
   Here, they do not howl.
They know by instinct
   that if they see a man
—any man—they should run.

Duel

I.
There, under the mountain laurel,
the mortal cracks inch-wide
and shell-long, the snapping turtle
had died, it appeared, not an hour
before I came across it. No flies
yet, the blood at its beak still wet,
and the gaze—if you'd call it that—
seemingly awake, enough for me to fear
I might be called on by some
imagined obligation to finish the job.
But neither the broken ash branch
nor my hesitant shoe triggered a twitch.
This stretch of mountain road,
pockmarked, something between
aggressive gravel and pothole,
acquitted speed, and the sheer size of the thing,
bigger than the mailbox above it,
excused blind carelessness.
The driver either had to swerve
or not swerve, as the people
observed in the study swerved
or didn't swerve in order to hit
or miss the tiny rubber turtles
the students had planted on the road. Men
three times more likely than women
to go out of their way for the kill.

II.
And in the movie, the trucker
stalking the man he wants to kill
has no face—it's not just that we don't see it:

he's a pure destroying force, evil,
if we still use that word. So at the end,
when the truck accelerates
through Dennis Weaver's car
and over the cliff, and the tanker's carcass
falls and twists in the canyon dust,
the trucker doesn't actually die
and instead haunts us. That shade
craving my daughter, my wife.
While the body hemorrhaging
on the running path: that's mine,
and the boys who shot it "just bored."
"What other animal but man
kills for fun," a friend asks,
and I remember my Lab
emerging from the hemlocks,
groundhog dangling from her mouth.
I yelled no, but the head hung limp,
the fat neck already snapped,
and my good dog's tail was going back
and forth, expressing, despite my protest,
what I knew was happiness.

A Variation on the Same

We had moved to the mountains the night before.
    So much sadness that first night, and darkness too:
no streetlamps—no streets, really, and the lone neighbor's house
    hundreds of yards away, dim as a new moon.

When the cows in the pasture woke me early,
    much too early it seemed, I left our bed,
Chelsea sleeping, her nipple halfway in the baby's mouth
    (dream feeding, we call it), and stumbled over our boxes
in the living room to go for a walk down the road
    where I came across the turtle:

        the broken shell, a beautiful ceramic luster
        of yellows and greens stressed by the fierce morning sun,
        militaristic ridges up the spine, too,
        a little like a terracotta helmet,
            and the cracks so deep
        they reminded me of the fissures
        of a cartoon earthquake.

        The couple of eggs the vehicle (car? truck?)
        had pressed out of her glistened with mucus in the gravel.

The fear I felt, different than the fear I would have felt
        had the thing been alive—

the unconscious holding
of my breath, as if all death were contagious,
which I guess it is.

    But why this urge to know
who aimed the wheel, and why he or she—no,

it was a he, I'm sure—did it? That face obscured
by a white sunbeam glancing off a windshield
I'll never see for sure.
                        And is the human delight
in the pain of others that far from suffering
because another suffers? I watched that other face,
the turtle's, its eyes and mouth open as if about to answer,
wet blood brimming at her jaw.

Reverberations

Twenty-some wires glued to her scalp,
  my eighteen-month-old daughter slept
    as I cradled her in a dim exam room,
our sole light the computer that mapped her brain activity—
  a digital needle scrawling a spastic cursive
    I couldn't read but studied anyway.

Now, months after getting the call that told us
  all was well, no signs of epilepsy,
    our hillside shudders, sending the pot rack
clanging like an angry wind chime. Then it ends.
  I survey our house, find no damage,
    not even a toppled chair, let alone a fissured wall.

Thankful for a disaster without consequence,
  I think of those vigilant instruments
    not far away, their jagged scribbles calmed
to the steady lines of this stillness I stand in.
  Outside, meanwhile, dogs howl at the inscrutable dark,
    which for all they know is about to move again.

Someone Takes a Pine Tree Apart

Because this summer the seventy-year-old pines
the original residents planted
have started falling on the neighborhood's houses,
splitting some as easily as cardboard boxes,
many mornings have begun like this one,
with a man climbing to the top branches,
a chainsaw dangling from a rope around his waist.

Today, it's our tree, one of the tallest for miles,
anchored to the drought-crumbled soil
by rotting roots. There's something artistic,
almost, about the way he dismembers
the very thing that holds him up,
the shorn branches more sinking than falling
as workers on the ground lower them by rope.
A hard-to-place sadness, too, in watching
as the trunk flails with each loss like an animal
trying to reach some unreachable pain.
Think a lanced bull. Think . . . No, there are things
that aren't like other things. And this is one.

All morning I've watched as these men,
whose language I don't understand, slowly dismantle
the risks necessity gives them. Soon,
they'll haul away all evidence of their work,
save for the huge stump ground to a blond dust
and a couple of abstractions: absence
and the feeling of safety when the wind picks up
and the rain weakens the soil, the once-hard ground.

Critique and Rebuttal

You're born, you suffer, you die. Then?
You're forgotten. At best the hypothetical
museum that unearths and houses your bones
(a fragment of your jaw, say) survives
a few centuries and doesn't crumble
until everything else does. Can you name
your grandfather's grandmother?
Nothing after. That drywall house
you've decorated with pictures
from occasional vacations where you ate
expensive cuts of meat, and mistook,
for brief moments, some lamplight over a river
as a sign of forgiveness for your wrongs:
oblivion bowls that little house over
well after the pictures have been taken down
and the new tenants move in and paint
over the color you said was perfect.
Nothing after. The new dog sniffs
the old dog's collar and we make up the rest.

✦

Not just some lamplight, and not just a river,
it was the Seine for one thing, and we stayed
a few doors down from where Matisse lived
when he painted *A Glimpse of Notre-Dame*.
On the night before our last night,
we sat on the steps to the riverwalk
that appear in that painting and waved at the boats
and kissed and clumsily took pictures
of ourselves. And because we were full

but not too full, and because we were drunk
but not too drunk, and because we had to
say goodbye to the city but not until tomorrow
and because the open shutter on the periphery
would be a mistake if the painting were
a photograph but because it *is* a painting,
we could walk back across the bridge
and up to our apartment to look
for those somber colors (I named one *cello blue,*
she called another *tempest green*),
then, before making love, we backed away
from the window, keeping our eyes on it,
as you might retreat, carefully, from something
you've balanced that shouldn't fall but will.

CODA

A Lasting Sickness

Five nights into fever, you lie in bed
as your parents, urgent, move about you
in the soft, almost birthday-candle-dim light.
If you're in pain, you won't remember,
though the fever's so high
it's likely you've reached that euphoric state
in which the dying or near-dying
see the oblong silhouettes of angels,
hear the shapeless voices of the dead.
Instead, you see your mother
watching you, along with a vigil
of good soldiers: the stuffed bears,
the purple rabbit, the papier-mâché parrot
perched on a painted hanger.
Your father plunges a washcloth
again into a mixing bowl of ice water,
brings it to your head, and you fall
back asleep to the sounds of your own
being cared for. If you were the boy
who remembers this well after
forgetting the cause, if it haunts you
like, say, unrepeatable pleasure
or a good dream you've never learned
to disbelieve, so that each sickness—
pneumonia at eighteen, shingles
at twenty-three—reminds you
of what others have done for you
and what others will do, their hands
working your clammy wrists and brow,
kneading the minty balm again and again
into your chest, if you began to believe,

as the boy did, that the world
not only acknowledges your suffering,
but turns to soothe it—what choice
would you have but to love that world
you so appallingly don't understand?

ACKNOWLEDGMENTS

Poems from this manuscript have appeared in the following publications:

32 Poems: "Time for Such a Word"; *Allegheny Review* (30th anniversary issue): "Sharpened Skates"; *Birmingham Poetry Review:* "'A Culture,'" "Saint Lucia," and "Two Angels"; *Ecotone:* "Butterfly Soup"; *Five Points:* "The Sap Gone Out"; *Green Mountains Review:* "Displacement," "An Explanation of Romanticism," "It Only Brings Me Sorrow," and "Protestant Elegy"; *Grist:* "Esteesee"; *Mead: The Magazine of Literature and Libations:* "Lessons"; *Missouri Review:* "Critique and Rebuttal," "A Lasting Sickness," "Portrait of the Self as Skunk Cabbage," "Smerdyakov with a Guitar," and "Someone Takes a Pine Tree Apart"; *New England Review:* "Natural Grief" and "The Reddened Flower, the Erotic Bird"; *New Haven Review:* "Late Coleridge" and "The Problem with Poems that Describe Love"; *New Ohio Review:* "The Crypt on the Rock," "My Keats Year," "One Pearl," and "Reciprocal"; *New Republic:* "Fringe Tree"; *[PANK]:* "To My Lover's Ex-Husband"; *Pleiades:* "Dispute"; *Rattle:* "At the Artists' Colony," "Nostos," and "The Reality Auction"; *storySouth:* "After Bashō" and "Basil"; *Southern Review:* "Duel" and "Oysters"; *Tampa Review:* "Fields and Ledges"; *Terminus:* "Gratis."

"An Existential Bear" appeared in *The Best New Poets 2015.*

"Fringe Tree," "Natural Grief," and "The Reddened Flower, the Erotic Bird" also appeared in *The Southern Poetry Anthology, Volume V: Georgia.*

Much gratitude to my teachers Christopher Bakken, David Bottoms, Mark Doty, Tony Hoagland, Jim Pipkin, and Adam Zagajewski, and my impeccable readers Katie Chaple, Travis Denton, Peter Hyland, Charlotte Pence, and Emily Schulten. I owe a debt to Paul Otremba, whose friendship and poetry sparked my thinking about Coleridge's conversation poems.
I am also grateful to the Community of Writers at Squaw Valley and the Sewanee Writers' Conference for their support. Thank you to my parents, my daughter, and particularly my wife, Chelsea Rathburn, without whom not one of these poems could have been written or revised. And special thanks to Claudia Emerson, who made this book possible.

www.ingramcontent.com/pod-product-compliance
Lightning Source LLC
Chambersburg PA
CBHW030121170426
43198CB00009B/700